English Rivi

GLOBAL GEOP

CW00406269

WALKS ALONG THE
SOUTH WEST
COAST PATH

Melanie Border & Ruth Luckhurst

EXMOUTH TO DARTMOUTH

COASTAL
PUBLISHING

A Coastal Publishing Book

Editor Alison Moss
Design Jonathan Lewis
Publishing Manager Susan Sutterby

First published in 2011 by Coastal Publishing
The Studio
Puddletown Road
Wareham
Dorset BH20 6AE

T: 01929 554195
E: enquiries@coastalpublishing.co.uk
www.coastalpublishing.co.uk
Coastal Publishing is a Sillson Communications Ltd Company

ISBN 978-1-907701-01-6

British Library Cataloguing-in-Publication Data
A catalogue record for this book is available from the British Library.

Printed and bound in China.

Front cover image: View towards the Mew Stone from Berry Head.

With great thanks to the South West Coast Path Team's partners
and Torbay Coast and Countryside Trust who manage the Coast
Path. With thanks also to John Risdon for his historical knowledge,
and for all donated photographs, in particular from Chris Slack
(www.chrisslack.com) Terry Hurt (www.terryhurtphotography.com)

Image Acknowledgements
(key: t:top, m:middle, b:bottom, l:left, r:right, c:centre)
Images in this book are copyright of the photographers and artists.

Cover Tina Edgell; 4 Philip Halstead; 5tr Rudolph Guldner; 8t, 15tr,
59bl Terry Hurt; 8b, 9br 9tr Teignbridge District Council; 14t Andy
Emmett; 15br, 19mr Andy Hay (rspb-images.com); 18t David Ayres;
18br TCCT; 22tl, 23tr, 26t, 27b, 38t, 49m, 52/53dps English Riviera
Tourism Company; 23b Stuart Murdoch; 26br D. Larkin; 32t, 39tr,
43b, 48t, 52tr, 58/59dps Chris Slack; 33br, 39br Melanie Border; 42t,
42b, 59br Ruth Luckhurst; 48br Elizabeth Aston; 53tr Nigel
Smallbones; 62/63dps SWCP/Paul Roberts; 62t National Trust Picture
Library/David Noton; 63tl Geoff Bonell.

English Riviera

GLOBAL GEOPARK

Conserving our past,
sustaining our future

LOTTERY FUNDED

South West Coast Path

NATIONAL TRAIL

COASTAL
PUBLISHING

CONTENTS

There is a whole world of new experiences waiting to be discovered along the South West Coast Path between Exmouth and Dartmouth. Whether you have a specialist interest or simply want to escape from the daily grind, the walks in this book will give you the chance to enjoy a breath of fresh air while at the same time learning something about the fascinating geology, wildlife, heritage and culture that have come together to make up this stunning landscape. What's more, there are some great pubs and cafés to refresh you along the way.

The majority of the walks follow the South West Coast Path – look out for the acorn symbol on signage along the way – a smaller number head off inland to take in beautiful woods and rolling farmland.

Walks 1 to 3 are set against the backdrop of the beautiful Dawlish Warren National Nature Reserve, Brunel's famous railway line and the towns of Teignmouth and Dawlish, with red cliffs, rare birds and views towards the Jurassic Coast to enjoy.

Walks 4 to 14 fall within the English Riviera

Thatcher Rock, Torquay.

View towards Dartmouth.

Global Geopark. The English Riviera has a superb landscape and natural history, with its mosaic of headlands, coastal cliffs, rocky islands and sheltered coves interwoven by seafront proms and bustling harbour areas waiting to be explored. Despite its mostly urban setting, this area contains one of the highest concentrations of protected geological sites in the UK. This rich geological heritage has influenced the area's remarkable marine and terrestrial biodiversity and shaped its diverse human history, from the earliest cave dwellers at Kents Cavern through to the millions of visitors the area welcomes today. It is this legacy that has led to international recognition and designation as a Global Geopark. This places the English Riviera in a global partnership alongside some of the most interesting and stunning places of natural beauty in the world, in countries such as Australia, Brazil, China, Iran and Malaysia.

Three of the Geopark's main visitor centres are included in walks in this book: Kents Cavern (Walk 6), The Seashore Centre (Walk 8) and Berry Head (Walk 14).

Walks 15 to 17 follow the more rugged coastline of the South Devon Area of Outstanding Natural Beauty, leading the walker on a journey from the Second World War back in time to the Civil War.

Two of the walks take in fascinating National Trust properties: the beautiful house and gardens of Greenway, holiday home of the famous crime writer Agatha Christie (Walk 11) and the Art Deco home of the D'Oyly Carte family at Coleton Fishacre (Walk 16).

The walks vary in length and difficulty but all of them are circular, with the exception of Walk 8, where a bus or ferry will get you back to the starting point.

Public Transport

The South West is well served by major trunk roads (M5, A303, A30) and the starting points of the walks are served by a network of A and B roads. Car parks (the majority of which are pay and display) are marked on the maps.

There are regular train services to Exmouth, Dawlish, Torquay and Paignton and a good network of bus routes. Details of bus and train services are available at www.traveline.info, or by telephoning the Traveline on +44 (0) 871 200 22 33, or via Stagecoach at www.stagecoachbus.com.

For details of ferry services operating between Torquay and Brixham visit www.greenwayferry.co.uk

For ferry services operating between Kingswear and Dartmouth visit www.dartmouth.org.uk/Details/The-Dartmouth-Lower-Ferry.

Dawlish

Dawlish Warren

Start/Finish

P

Langstone
Rock

DAWLISH WARREN

WALK 1 – Dawlish Warren

Distance	6.5 miles (10.5km)
Estimated time	2¾ hours
Difficulty	● ● ○ ○ ○
Ascent	217ft (66m)
Map	OS Explorer Map 110
Starting point	SX 979787

Notes: This is an easy walk on level roads and paths, starting in Dawlish Warren National Nature Reserve and taking in wonderful views along the coast before passing some fascinating buildings in this Regency resort. Part of the route travels along the sea wall; if the weather is bad or the tide high, you will need to take the inland route on the other side of the railway line.

Beginning at Dawlish Warren Railway Station, head left under the railway arch and into the Dawlish Warren National Nature Reserve. Going through the car park, pick up the footpath at the far end and follow it past the Visitor Centre and on through the reserve as it curves around to the right to meet the beach. On the beach turn right and walk down to the sea wall. Visitors are welcome to walk in the dunes surrounding the Visitor Centre, but there is no public access to the golf course, or to the mudflats to the north and west. Other restrictions apply elsewhere according to the time of year and the state of the tide. Dogs are allowed in some areas, but should be kept on a short lead. Please observe the guidelines displayed in the reserve, as they are designed to preserve this as a special place.

Head south along the sea wall and cliff-side path towards the red stacks at Langstone Rock. Continue south on the South West Coast Path alongside the railway line to Dawlish Station.

Towards Exmouth
from Dawlish Warren.

On an early summer morning when the sea is calm, sometimes dolphins can be seen swimming along this part of the coast.

From the station car park continue down the road with the sea to your left, then turn right along Brookdale Terrace and enter Brunswick Place. Note the fine Regency houses as you walk here. Cross over the road bridge and take the path marked 'Manor Grounds' along the left bank of the brook. Go under the arch of the building in front and pass through the Manor Grounds, with the brook still to your right. At the far end, cross the little bridge over the mill leat and go along the path.

Turn left into Church Street and go through the gate to follow the path through Newhay. By the Newhay Falls you will see another sluice and the junction where the leat comes off the brook from the Aller Valley. Go through the gate and continue ahead until you reach the road, turning right up Aller Hill and continuing to Weech Road. Turn right onto Weech Road and carry on to the High Street. Keep going until you reach the crossroads, then continue straight ahead, on the main road to Exeter, for a little over half a mile, passing a church on your left. Cross over at the pedestrian crossing and carry on until you pass the Post Office on your right. Turn right onto Warren Road, then immediately onto the path signed straight ahead. Continue along this cliff-top path, back to Dawlish Warren Station.

The Exe Estuary is south-west England's most important wildfowl and wader feeding area, with up to 20,000 wildfowl and waders of twenty different species. The brent geese and black-tailed godwits in particular, are of international importance, as are the avocets, forming one of Britain's largest winter flocks.

Male sand lizard at
Dawlish Warren.

As many as 8,000 wading birds rest at Warren Point at high tide, and the site supports over 600 plant species, including the rare Sand crocus (unofficially known as the Warren crocus), which is only found in one other place in the UK. New species are still being discovered here, such as the petalwort, a very rare liverwort.

Birds in the reserve include thousands of oystercatchers and dunlins, with several hundred ringed and grey plovers and curlews, and a few dozen knots, sanderlings and turnstones. Larger species roost in flocks along the tideline, while the smaller birds gather on the mud and gravel. From time to time grey herons, kingfishers and even peregrines can be seen fishing in the area, and little egrets sometimes fly through. Onshore, a short-eared owl occasionally sits

Warren crocus.

in the dunes near the point, and in hard weather a snow bunting might be seen on the beach.

Dawlish

With a rich history going back to pre-Roman salt makers, Dawlish has some fascinating buildings.

The current Dawlish Station dates from the 1870s, but at the far end of the car park the remains of one of the pumping houses designed by Isambard Kingdom Brunel for his ingenious but ill-fated Atmospheric Railway can be found (see page 14).

In Brunswick Place you will see the buildings and huge wheel of the former Strand or Torbay Mill (now a restaurant). The waterwheel is 30 feet in diameter and of pitchback type (the most common kind of waterwheel, where the used water flows away in the same direction as the wheel). The brick-built launder (trough) has been restored in recent years and the wheel now turns again.

At the bottom of Badlake Hill there are several attractive thatched cottages, as well as a former cider-making farm and malthouse. There is a Victorian Gothic drinking fountain set in the corner of a wall a little way beyond, and the grey stone public library, further on again, was originally built as a soup kitchen. In the High Street is the site of the former Ferris Brewery, which made beers from local barley and mineral waters. The marble bottle-stoppers they used can still sometimes be found in the town.

TEIGNMOUTH

Holcombe

Teignmouth

Start/Finish

P

Hole Head

WALK 2 – Teignmouth

Distance	4.25 miles (6.9km)
Estimated time	2 hours
Difficulty	●● ● ● ●
Ascent	658ft (200m)
Map	OS Explorer Map 110
Starting point	SX 945732

Notes: A walk along the sea wall returns via inland paths and quiet lanes to Eastcliff Park, a designated Area of Great Landscape Value. There are short stretches of steep ascent and descent, and the walk should not be attempted at times of high tides or stormy weather. In summer parking may be restricted, in which case leave your car just a few minutes walk away, at Teignmouth Station.

From the Lookout Station on Teignmouth seafront, turn left onto the South West Coast Path and follow it along the sea wall to the steps at Hole Head. Go down the steps and follow Smuggler's Lane steeply uphill to the Teignmouth Road (A379). Turn right and walk to Windward Lane, on your right, to pick up the path on your left. Follow it around the back of the headland and steeply downhill, alongside the railway line, before it curves left, inland, up to the road again.

Turn left and walk to the footpath sign pointing between houses on the opposite side of the road. Take this footpath and follow it through fields to the road beyond. Turn left and walk downhill to the sharp left-hand bend. Continue straight ahead on the lane to the right, travelling between fields at the back of Holcombe to drop down via Oak Hill Cross Road to Teignmouth Road. Cross the road and go straight down Cliff Road, picking up the footpath a little way beyond on the right, through Mules Park to the seafront.

WALK 2

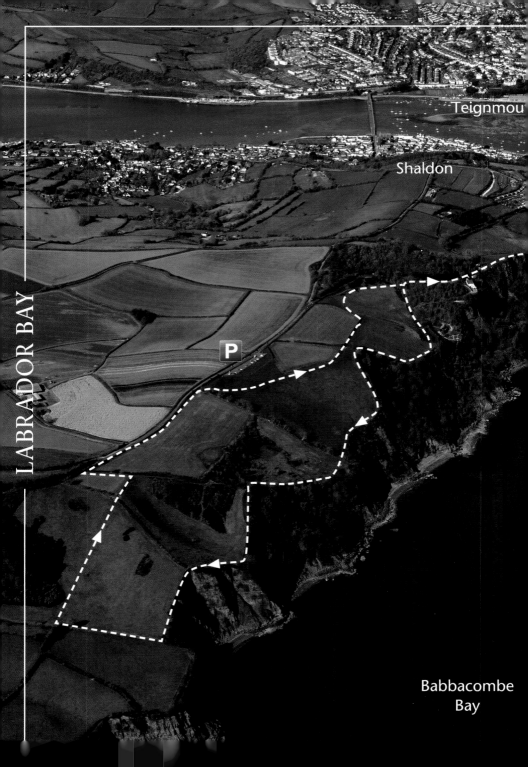

LABRADOR BAY

Teignmou

Shaldon

P

Babbacombe
Bay

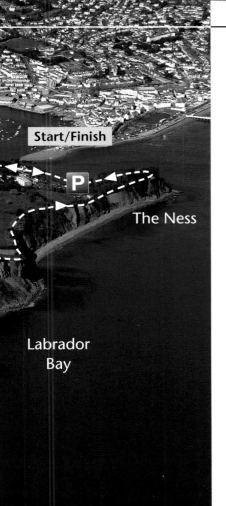

Start/Finish

P

The Ness

Labrador
Bay

WALK 3 – Labrador Bay

Distance	5.25 miles (8.5km)
Estimated time	3 hours
Difficulty	● ● ● ● ○
Ascent	1,319ft (402m)
Map	OS Explorer Map 110
Starting point	SX 937722

Notes: A strenuous but rewarding walk with stunning coastal views, passing around the headland at The Ness, then looping through the RSPB Nature Reserve at Labrador Bay, where the once-rare cirl bunting can be seen in the bushes and shy roe deer are sometimes glimpsed. The route passes through farmland where stock graze so can be wet and muddy in winter, requiring good footwear. Dogs must be kept under control.

From the beach at Shaldon, take the South West Coast Path to the headland. Climb The Ness and turn southwards around the coastline, dropping through trees to the car park beyond. Bear left and carry on above Ness Cove, up the steps and past the pitch-and-putt fields, climbing steeply to the A379. Turn left and walk a short way to turn left again, onto the Coast Path, up and down around the edge of fields (ignoring the path to the right at the edge of the wood).

After about a mile, turn right onto a footpath leading uphill until you reach the next path, just before the trees. Turn right and follow this path uphill, towards the A379. Turn right before the top and walk about 300 yards. Here the footpath drops to the right and travels below the Labrador Bay car park before returning to the road. Turn right again and walk back to the Coast Path on the hillside below, to retrace your steps past the golf course to The Ness and Shaldon.

WALK 3

Teignmouth Pier.

The railway line here was once part of Isambard Kingdom Brunel's innovative Atmospheric Railway of 1847–8. Instead of being drawn by locomotives in the traditional fashion, the carriages were attached to pipes that propelled them by means of suction. Steam-powered pumps in a series of engine houses along the route were used to create a vacuum through the pipes. Unfortunately the system was sealed with leather flaps, which deteriorated rapidly due to a combination of saltwater spray and hungry rats gnawing through the tallow used to keep the leather valves supple. As a result it was difficult to maintain the necessary pressure in the pipes and the trains were forever breaking down, requiring third-class passengers to get out and push!

A further problem was that there was no telegraph system to warn the pumping stations when a train would be late, so they had to empty the pipes according to a strict timetable, whether a train was approaching or not. The frequent breakdowns meant that the resultant unnecessary pumping made the whole system very expensive to run. The railway's accounts for 1848 suggest that the running costs were more than twice those incurred when a locomotive was used and by the end of that year it was decided to use these instead.

The tunnel in Smuggler's Lane is known as Parson's Tunnel, after the Parson and Clerk rocks off the headland. According to local legend, an ambitious parson from an inland parish had high hopes of succeeding the Bishop of Exeter, who lay dying in Dawlish. To further his cause, he paid the bishop regular visits, guided by his parish clerk. One day the two lost their way in thick fog and spent hours wandering around in the heavy rain. The parson, a man of uncertain temper, became angry and berated his unfortunate clerk for his incompetence, assuring him that he'd rather be guided by the Devil.

Stumbling upon a peasant a short while later, they allowed him to lead them to a tumbledown cottage, where a riotous crowd was enjoying a lively drinking session. Warmed and soothed by a good meal and rather too much ale, the parson and his clerk were somewhat the worse for wear when news arrived at dawn that the bishop had died. Throwing themselves upon their horses, the two men tried to set forth, but the horses would not move. Suddenly the crowd of merrymakers turned into leering demons, hooting horribly at the parson's plight, and the cottage disappeared in a puff of smoke.

Realising, too late, that he had indeed been guided by the Devil, the parson found himself stranded in the sea, with his clerk also adrift some distance away. In that instant, they were both turned to stone, and there they stand to this day.

The Parson and Clerk rocks were once part of the headland, until the erosive action of heavy seas on the rocks weakened cracks in its structure initially to form arches, now fallen to leave stacks. The cliff face beside the tunnel shows a rock type for which this part of the coastline is known: a breccia (one rock – in this case a sandstone – containing angular fragments of another) from the Permian Period.

The Ness (see Walk 3) is a prominent landmark on this part of the coastline, with its high red cliffs of Permian sandstone

Across the River Teign from Shaldon.

topped by woodland planted in Victorian times. Running beneath the headland is a smugglers' tunnel leading to Ness Cove. There is also an old lime kiln on the beach, once used for making fertiliser from local limestone that was brought here by ship.

Cirl buntings can sometimes be seen in the bushes around Labrador Bay. Small migratory birds, such as whitethroats and blackcaps are more common, as are ravens and peregrine falcons. Looking out to sea, you might be lucky enough to spot a pod of dolphins or gannets gliding and diving headfirst into the water to catch fish.

Higher Gabwell

Walk 4 – Maidencombe

Distance	3.7 miles (5.9km)
Estimated time	2 hours
Difficulty	● ● ● ○ ○
Ascent	495ft (151m)
Map	OS Explorer Map 110
Starting point	SX 923674

Notes: Starting at Watcombe Beach car park, reached via the A379 (Teignmouth Road), this walk provides panoramic vistas over Babbacombe Bay and Lyme Bay with a chance to view the unspoilt countryside that borders Torquay.

From the car park, head over the stile onto the South West Coast Path in a northerly direction. The path wends its way across undulating ground known as the Valley of the Rocks. When the path splits follow the waymarked Coast Path down into Maidencombe.

At Maidencombe, an attractive cove is accessible from the Coast Path where there is a café (seasonal opening) or, if preferred, refreshment can be taken in the thatched pub in the village before continuing.

From the village the Coast Path goes north, burrowing its way through a natural arbour of vegetation and wild flowers, with intervening vistas of sea, sky and red sandstone cliffs, for the best part of a mile before reaching the Torbay boundary with Teignbridge, indicated by a stile, just beyond Herring Cove. Here the route strikes off inland, at right angles to the Coast Path, climbing up over meadow. The view from the top of the hill provides an inspiring and elevated view over Lyme Bay to be enjoyed before the return to Maidencombe. The path heads back over the fields, crossing the track

WALK 4

Fields at Maidencombe.

that leads down towards Mackerel Cove, until it joins another track leading to Steep Hill. Turn left downhill.

Head out of the village along Rock House Lane past the village orchard. This short but steep climb up brings the route onto a section of country track that then joins once again with the Coast Path to take the walker back over the Valley of the Rocks to the starting point. The great sandstone cliff face that bears down over the path adjacent to the car park is known as Giant Rock. This was a considerable attraction in Victorian times and would have been even more spectacular when the area was open downland without tree cover.

The dramatic red rocks that are exposed in the cliffs at Maidencombe were formed in a desolate desert environment just north of the equator approximately 280 million years ago, during the Permian Period. This was a time when, in dry periods, wind-blown sands were deposited and, during rare violent storms, flash floods swept stones and rocks down desert valleys, out into an open plain. Here within the English Riviera Global Geopark these deposits of sandstones and breccias are internationally significant. They actually form the starting point of the geological sequence also designated along the coast as the Jurassic Coast World Heritage Site, which on a clear day can be viewed stretching into the distance to the north.

Ruby Red cattle grazing at Maidencombe.

Finer sediments were deposited as clays, and the deep red clays discovered around the Watcombe area led to the development of Torquay's famous terracotta industry, once regarded as the finest in England. The first pottery opened in 1867 and produced a wide variety of items, including the famous Devon Motto Ware. The dark red and brown colours of the products were obtained by mixing local red clay with manganese, Dorset clay and flint. Torquay Museum holds a fine collection of these terracotta pieces.

Nestling in a sheltered hollow amidst dramatic coastal scenery, the historic settlement of Maidencombe featured in the Domesday Book as Medenecombe. The majority of its buildings cluster around Steep Hill and Rock House Lane, and still standing today is the fourteenth-century Court with its associated dovecote and Judas tree, thought to have been brought back from the Lebanon as a sapling in the mid-sixteenth century. The combination of red sandstone and thatch still continues to provide the warmth and tradition that characterised many a South Devon village or farmstead. The setting looks idyllic today, but in centuries past Maidencombe would have been well known to smugglers.

Cirl Bunting

Cirl buntings (right) were once so common in the English countryside that they were known as the 'village bunting'. Intensive farming methods reduced their numbers dramatically during the latter half of the twentieth century, however, and since then the Royal Society for the Protection of Birds (RSPB) has been leading a project working with Devon farmers to find ways of reviving them. Planting spring barley then leaving the stubble until the following spring provides winter food, and grazing with cattle and Dartmoor ponies keeps the vegetation under control and encourages grasshoppers and crickets, also part of a bunting's diet. The male bird has a black mask over a yellow head and an olive-green rump, while the female is less colourful, her brown, rather plain plumage helping her to remain safely camouflaged on the nest hidden in the thick hedgrows.

Labrador Bay (see Walk 3) was bought by the RSPB in 2008, while the farmland

around Maidencombe is cared for by Torbay Coast and Countryside Trust. Both organisations use traditional farming methods to provide a habitat for cirl buntings and make this a hotspot for the bird in Devon. Throughout South Devon the strategy has been so successful that cirl buntings have made a dramatic recovery from less than 120 pairs in 1989 to over 850 pairs in 2009. Other farmland birds, such as the skylark, also benefit from this management. Rare plants such as weasel's snout and wild pansies have been making a comeback too.

Babbacombe

BABBACOMBE

Start/Finish

P

Short cut

Walls Hill

Long Quarry Point

Babbacombe
Cliff Railway

Oddicombe
Beach

Babbacombe
Beach

Walk 5 – Babbacombe

Distance	2.25 miles (3.6km)
Estimated time	1 hour
Difficulty	●●●○○
Ascent	331ft (101m)
Map	OS Explorer Map 110
Starting point	SX 929653

Notes: The Babbacombe Cliff Railway can be used as an unusual start to your journey, or follow the route backwards to save a steep climb up from Babbacombe Beach. The Cliff Railway operates daily March to October, weekends only November and December, but is closed January and February.

From the car park behind the Old Coach House pub on Walls Hill Road walk along Babbacombe Downs Road to Babbacombe Downs, one of the highest cliff-top promenades in Britain. Overlooking Babbacombe Bay and Lyme Bay, the Downs are approximately 90 metres (300 feet) above sea level and, on a clear day, provide a panoramic view across roughly 30 miles of coastline beyond East Devon and into Dorset.

At the northern end of the Downs, just past the small bronze memorial statue of Lady Mount Temple, follow the South West Coast Path down to Oddicombe Beach, or take a ride down on the cliff railway. Follow the path along the edge of the shore towards Babbacombe Beach. At the far end is an award-winning gastro pub, the Cary Arms, which is owned by the de Savary family. Behind the pub the Coast Path heads off up into woodland to Walls Hill. A stroll around the headland will bring you back to the starting point.

WALK 5

Babbacombe Cliff Railway.

base of the cliff between Oddicombe and Babbacombe Beach. Looking back up the slope, the division between the limestone and slate is marked by a line of small springs. Meanwhile, the cliff behind Oddicombe Beach, reveals a major fault movement: a massive block of red breccia has dropped down between the older Devonian rocks, looking like a keystone.

In 1890 Sir George Newnes, MP, saw the potential of using the fault line to create a cliff railway connecting Babbacombe Downs with the beach, but it was some years before the idea became reality. The cliff railway was not opened by the mayor until 1926. Today, it is one of only sixteen funicular railways still functioning in Britain.

Compared to limestone, the red sandstone and breccias are soft and more vulnerable to the natural erosive qualities of the sea, rain and frost, leaving them prone to rockfalls and landslides. A major rockfall occurred early in 2010 at the northern end of Oddicombe Beach; this area of the beach has been closed to the public since 2002 because of the cliff's instability. Even from a safe distance it is easy to see the next chunk of rock waiting to crash to the beach below. After a fall the sea temporarily turns blood red, until the debris dissipates. However, a truly bloody tale lurks just around the coast.

In 1884 a man named John Lee was accused of murdering his employer, a wealthy lady called Emma Keyse, who lived on the coast at Babbacombe Bay, near Torquay. Having resided at The Glen in Babbacombe most of her life, Emma Keyse was a well-known member of this respectable community. Her mother even had Royal connections, hosting visits from Princess (later Queen) Victoria and the

Here at Babbacombe Downs steely-grey Devonian limestones contrast with red Permian sandstones and breccias to create a spectacular view. The setting looks tranquil today, but scratch beneath the surface and there are some dramatic tales to be told. Layers of sediments are always deposited one on top of the other, with the most recent at the very top, yet in this area incredible forces have dramatically twisted and tilted the layers, pushing them out of sequence. As a result of plate tectonics the older pale limestone has been pushed over the dark slates, which are actually younger. You can see the slates from the coast path along the

Duchess of Kent on several occasions. Yet, in the early hours of 15 November 1884, Emma Keyse was discovered brutally murdered. Her throat had been cut, she had three wounds to her head and the murderer had also attempted to burn her body. The following year John Lee was convicted and was sent to be hanged at Exeter. However, on the scaffold the trapdoor failed to open three times, so it was decided that Lee should serve a life sentence in prison. Lee's story became known around the world and when he was released from prison he became a minor celebrity, known as John 'Babbacombe' Lee.

Out of loyalty to Emma and her mother, two local elderly sisters continued to live in the burnt-out wreckage of the cottage for over a year after the murder, until one of them died there in 1885, an eerie twist to the end of the tale.

Walls Hill limestone plateau sits high above the dramatically shaped Long Quarry Point, which was created by quarrying stone for Regency and Victorian development.

View from Babbacombe Downs.

Stone from nearby Petitor, with its marble-like effect when highly polished, was made into popular ornamental furnishings. Today the London Natural History Museum displays a Petitor marble table.

Walls Hill was home to an Iron Age hillfort 2,500 years ago, a defended headland where local people would have gathered when under attack. Today, in more peaceful times, a population of rare small blue butterflies has been recorded here following a reintroduction programme. This delicate creature relies on kidney vetch, a grassland plant that thrives on limestone.

Small Blue butterfly.

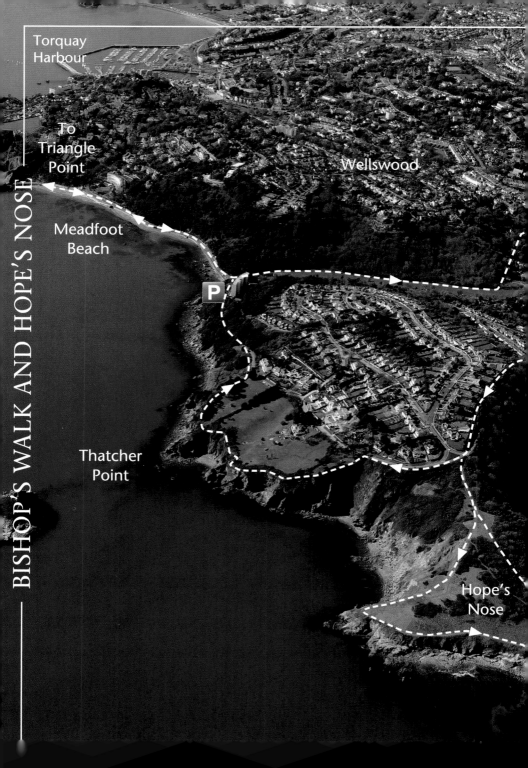

BISHOP'S WALK AND HOPE'S NOSE

Torquay Harbour

To Triangle Point

Meadfoot Beach

Wellswood

Thatcher Point

Hope's Nose

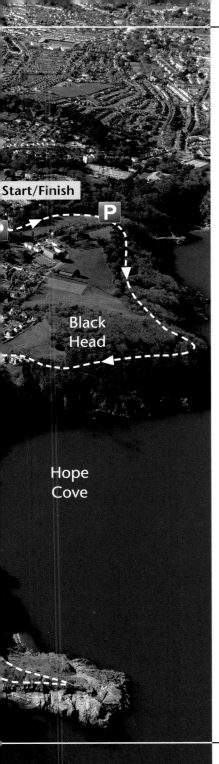

Start/Finish

Black Head

Hope Cove

Walk 6 – Bishop's Walk and Hope's Nose

Distance	2.85 miles (4.6km)
Estimated time	2 hours
Difficulty	● ● ● ○ ○
Ascent	331ft (101m)
Map	OS Explorer Map 110
Starting point	SX 935642

Notes: Allow more time if you would like to visit Kents Cavern, Britain's most important cave dwelling and a gateway visitor centre for the English Riviera Global Geopark. Open all year round, it offers regular guided tours, as well as having a restaurant and shop.

Starting from Kents Cavern car park, take the steps down to Ilsham Road and enter the field opposite. Stroll along the playing field towards Anstey's Cove. From the top corner of Anstey's Cove car park the South West Coast Path is clearly waymarked and strikes off around the coast following what is known as Bishop's Walk. However, first you may wish to head down the steep path to Anstey's Cove, which nestles between high cliffs and a thickly wooded hillside. Here you will find a café (seasonal opening hours).

Bishop's Walk ends where the Coast Path joins Ilsham Marine Drive. From here cross the road and turn left, where you continue on a raised path above the road. The Coast Path re-emerges onto Ilsham Marine Drive directly opposite the entrance to Hope's Nose. At this point you may wish to take a detour by crossing the road and heading over the stile to enjoy the spectacular views and superb geology of the Hope's Nose promontory. A downloadable geological trail exists for the headland

WALK 6

Long Quarry Point.

(www.englishrivierageopark.org.uk), but be warned, it is a steep and slippery climb in places and involves some scrambling along the shoreline.

If you do not wish to explore Hope's Nose continue along the Coast Path, which now runs along the northern side of the bay via Ilsham Marine Drive and sections of footpath towards Meadfoot Beach. Evergreen holm oak, a species of tree that was introduced by the Victorians, is common here. Once at the junction of Ilsham Marine Drive and Ilsham Road you can take a detour to enjoy the beach. There are toilets and a café (seasonal opening) at the southern end of the beach. Venturing past the café, a scramble to Triangle Point reveals spectacular marine Devonian fossils, but for those less adventurous there are some great fossils to be found all along Meadfoot Sea Road in the limestone sea wall. Retrace your steps back to the junction of Ilsham Marine Drive with Ilsham Road.

To continue, cross Ilsham Road and go over the green to the edge of the woods. Follow a footpath through the woods up the Ilsham Valley. This terminates at Kents

Cavern, a prehistoric cave with a remarkable history of ancient human occupation.

Kents Cavern is both a scheduled monument and a Site of Special Scientific Interest. Through its geology and archaeological finds, it reveals dramatic evidence of the Geopark's earliest inhabitants, over 500,000 years ago, and the pioneering work of Victorian explorers who uncovered the stories of its prehistoric past.

Bishop's Walk is named after Henry Phillpotts, who was Bishop of Exeter from 1831 until his death in 1869. In 1842, to escape the cholera-infected streets of

Marine Devonian coral fossil.

Exeter, Phillpotts built a grand Italianate-style mansion called Bishopstowe, which is today the Palace Hotel. Unsatisfied with his mansion, spectacular gardens and land overlooking Anstey's Cove, the bishop set about creating a path along the nearby cliffs. Here he would enjoy a regular breath of fresh air and time for contemplation.

After extensive and extravagant expansion, Bishopstowe was converted into a hotel in 1921. Like many of Britain's hotels, it was commandeered for use as a military hospital during the Second World War, but after two direct hits by German bombers the hospital was abandoned. It reopened as a hotel again in 1948.

Hope's Nose forms a delightful if small curving bay in which sailing ships could seek shelter in stormy conditions. It is possible that this hoped-for respite brought about the name of Tor Bay's most northerly promontory. The headland itself not only provides a spectacular vantage point but is an exceptional site for its geology and biodiversity. Rare limestone grassland plants carpet the steep slope down to the wave-cut platform, which reveals fantastic fossils of delicate corals from the ancient Devonian seas. Broken by the waves, these were washed between large sponge structures called stromatoporoids. Contorted by immense pressure as two continents collided roughly 300 million years ago, the limestone seen here is undulating and faulted. Minerals, deposited in the Permian or Triassic Period, including selenium, palladium and even gold, have been found here and this has made the site attractive to illegal collectors. However, a recovery project, led by experts from London's Natural History Museum, has rescued the remaining pods of gold and safeguarded the scientific value of these deposits. At the far south-east corner of the headland the raised beach, with embedded pebbles and fossilised marine shells, is evidence of past climate change.

Just offshore the view is punctuated by the two limestone islets of Thatcher Rock and Orestone (to the left). Colonies of guillemots and kittiwakes have made the islands their home. Careful observation of Orestone reveals further evidence of the pressure the limestone was subjected to where a huge fracture runs through the centre and the mass of limestone to the right of the fracture has been pushed up and folded over on itself.

WALK 6

Sea pinks at Thatcher Point.

Royal
Terrace
Gardens

Torquay
Harbour

P

Beacon
Cove

Peaked
Tor Cove

London Bridge

Daddyhole Plain

P

Start/Finish

Walk 7 – Daddyhole and Rock End

Distance	1.8 miles (3km)
Estimated time	1 hour
Difficulty	● ● ○ ○ ○
Ascent	265ft (78m)
Map	OS Explorer Map 110
Starting point	SX 928630

Notes: The views across the bay from Daddyhole Plain and secluded Rock End Walk are quite spectacular.

This walk starts at Daddyhole Plain, but beware, 'Daddy' is the old Devon term for the Devil, who locals used to think, lived in a cave at the base of the cliff. Follow the Coast Path in a south-westerly direction, as it hugs the shoreline, winding down towards Torquay Harbour. Just prior to reaching Peaked Tor Cove the path divides at the bottom of some steps. Detour left to view the iconic natural arch, London Bridge. At Peaked Tor Cove take time to explore where the Torbay Home Guard kept watch over the bay during the Second World War.

At Parkhill Road turn left towards the harbour, passing Beacon Cove, a ladies-only beach until 1903 and a favourite swimming spot for Agatha Christie as a young girl.

Cross the Millennium Bridge, which spans the entrance to the inner harbour. Turn right and walk around the harbour. It is difficult to believe that you are walking on what was once the mouth of the River Fleet. Today the river is hidden underground. At the Mallock Clock Tower head up Torwood Street to the traffic lights, then turn right onto Meadfoot Road. Take a right into Parkhill Road, then left onto Daddyhole Road, which takes you back to the starting point.

WALK 7

Torquay

Start/Finish

Paignton

Paignton Sands

Goodrington Sands

Saltern Cove

Broadsands Beach

Elberry Cove

Churston Cove

Brixham
Harbour

Brixham

Babbacombe Bay

Hope's Nose

Tor Bay

Walk 8 – Torquay Harbour to Brixham Harbour

Distance	8.4 miles (13.5km)
Estimated time	5 hours
Difficulty	● ● ● ○ ○
Ascent	335ft (102m)
Map	OS Explorer Map 110
Starting point	SX 918631

Notes: There are several stretches of footpath and pavement walking here as well as wilder places. Parking is available at Beacon Quay or the Harbour car park. The return journey is by bus or ferry (seasonal service), so check times before you leave.

From Torquay Harbour head across the Millennium Bridge, passing in front of the Pavilion. On the right are the Royal Terrace Gardens. It is worth heading up the steps to enjoy the spectacular view from the viewing platform.

Follow the promenade around the seafront, passing 800-year-old Torre Abbey which sits majestically back across the green. Continue on the seafront road (A3022). At Hollicombe turn into Hollicombe Park, veer to the right and in the far right-hand corner of the park head through the gate. Turn left over the railway bridge and then right to Preston Sands. At low tide it is possible to walk the whole length of Preston and Paignton Sands along the beach. At high tide a short section of pavement round the Redcliff Hotel links the two beaches. From the southern end of Paignton Sands follow the promenade to Paignton Harbour and Fairy Cove. Steps at the back of the beach go up to Cliff Road. Here turn left and then left again onto Roundham Head. The cliff walk on the southern side of the headland descends to Goodrington Beach.

WALK 8

Churston Cove at sunrise.

Between North Sands and South Sands you will find a range of facilities, including the Seashore Centre, a gateway site for the English Riviera Global Geopark.

If you are feeling adventurous when you reach the southern end of South Sands stay on the beach. At low tide only, it is possible to ramble over the rocks around to Saltern Cove. This section of coastline provides some spectacular insights into our geological past (download the Saltern Cove Geological Trail from www.englishrivierageopark.org.uk), but do not attempt to walk here unless you have checked tide times first. From Saltern Cove steps at the back of the beach take you up onto a grassy headland and from here you need to cross a bridge over the railway to rejoin the Coast Path.

Otherwise, at the end of South Sands go under the railway bridge and turn immediately left onto the Coast Path, which takes you over Sugarloaf Hill. Shortly after the caravan site turn left under the railway bridge to enjoy the view. Cross back under the railway line and turn left.

The path continues south, where steep steps take you down and under the viaduct towards Broadsands Beach. From the southern end of Broadsands Beach follow Walk 12 (page 44) until you reach Churston Cove.

When the Coast Path climbs steeply away from Churston Cove up through woodland and starts to level out, turn left through the gate waymarked Brixham. A short alleyway leads to Fishcombe Road. Turn left down to Fishcombe Cove and on through Battery Gardens, first used as a battery in 1586 in the war between England and Spain. From here the path to Brixham Harbour is clear.

Follow the waterfront around to the inner harbour. You can get back to Torquay via sea or land. The ferry service operates from May to October or take the No.12 bus from Brixham Bus Station.

The striking limestone headlands of Hope's Nose and Berry Head were formed south of the equator around 400 million years ago, when the whole area would have been under warm tropical seas, where corals thrived and trilobites scuttled across the seabed. The shells and skeletons of these creatures accumulated layer upon layer and were compressed over millions of years to form hard limestone.

Over the next 100 million years these rocks were folded and fractured as they were pushed northwards by plate tectonic processes, the dramatic results of which can be seen at various points along the coast.

Royal Terrace Gardens exist as the result of more recent dramatic earth movements with the formation of the Alps. Having crossed the entire South-West, it is here that a great tear in the earth's crust, the Sticklepath Fault, shows itself in the form of this jumbled cliff face, before it heads out to sea.

By 280 million years ago the English Riviera was at approximately the same latitude as the Sahara Desert today. This is when the red rocks now exposed around the inner areas of the bay were formed. Look closely around Roundham Head and the gently curving diagonal lines in the finer sandstone deposits reveal the profile of ancient wind-blown sand dunes, while the rocks and stones at the southern end of Goodrington Beach are evidence of flash floods. Sudden storms in distant mountains caused torrents of water to carry and then deposit a jumble of rocks and stones. Between Goodrington South Sands and Saltern Cove it is possible to find fossil evidence of life in the desert. A burrowing creature has left its mark in the form of rearranged sands and pebbles.

The hard limestone has withstood erosion for hundreds of thousands of years, acting as protective arms, while the less resistant sandstone rocks have been worn away. At the end of the last glacial period ice caps slowly melted, causing sea levels to rise. By 7,000 years ago the sea had risen to its present level, flooding woodland. Remnants of this sunken forest are sometimes revealed at low tide on Torre Abbey Sands and Goodrington Beach.

Today, Tor Bay's mix of sheltered sandy shores, rocky coves and rugged limestone cliffs backed by woodland and rolling farmland provides a range of important habitats within a relatively small area. It is difficult to imagine that not so long ago early humans would have been chasing mammoths over the cliffs, then competing with hyenas for the meat before heading back to the shelter of Kents Cavern.

Princess Pier, Torquay.

COCKINGTON

Link to Scadson Woods

Cockington

P Start/Finish

Link to South West Coast Path

Livermead Sands

Corbyn Head

Torre Abbey

Walk 9 – Cockington

Distance	3.75 miles (6km)
Estimated time	1½ hours
Difficulty	● ● ● ○ ○
Ascent	305ft (93m)
Map	OS Explorer Map 110
Starting point	SX 894638

Notes: Starting in the historic village of Cockington, this walk takes in green fields and wooded coombes with beautiful views down across this hidden valley, now a country park.

From the car park in the centre of the village turn right onto Cockington Lane. Follow the lane out of the village and past orchards. Where the lane turns uphill to the right, leave the road and continue straight ahead on the unsurfaced track to Horse Barton. From here head through the gate on the left. Passing Fruit Farm Copse on your left, follow the path around the head of the valley, turning left back down towards Cockington village, where there are signposts indicating Stantor Barton to the right. Where the path divides, take the right-hand option through the gate in a low stone wall. At the lane turn left for a very short stretch before heading through the gate on the right down to Warren Barn. Turn left along the edge of Manscombe Woods down to the Gamekeeper's Cottage. Once beyond the cottage head to the right, past three ponds and then through one of the original entrances to the estate, Lower Lodge. From here turn left to walk back through the village to the starting point.

From here it is only a short walk to Cockington Court which is today a vibrant centre for arts and crafts.

WALK 9

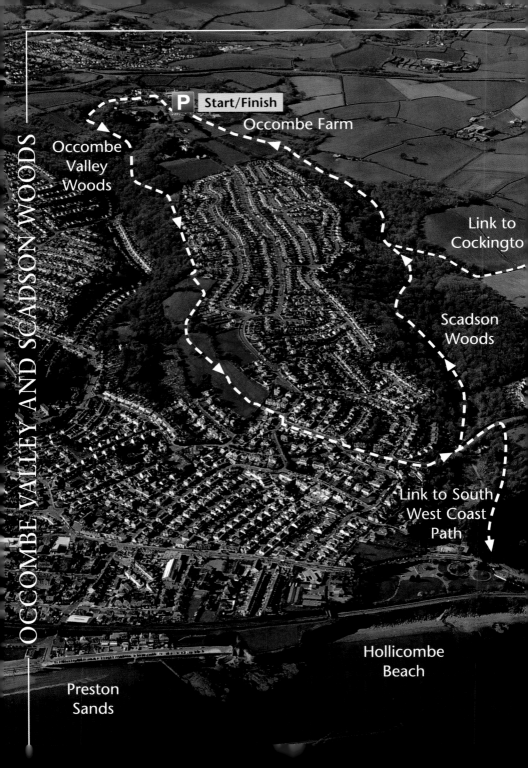

OCCOMBE VALLEY AND SCADSON WOODS

P Start/Finish

Occombe Farm

Occombe Valley Woods

Link to Cockingto

Scadson Woods

Link to South West Coast Path

Hollicombe Beach

Preston Sands

Walk 10 – Occombe Valley and Scadson Woods

Distance	3.1 miles (5km)
Estimated time	1½ hours
Difficulty	● ● ● ○ ○
Ascent	333ft (101m))
Map	OS Explorer Map 110
Starting point	SX 875632

Notes: There is a large car park at Occombe Farm and, of course, you can visit the farm and café there as a great start or end to your walk.

From Occombe Farm cross over Preston Down Road and just to the right you will see the waymark for Occombe Valley Woods. Head down the track and then through the gate into the woods. Follow the drovers' path until you come across a small wooden footbridge on the left. Cross the bridge and stay on this path. At the small area of open grassland walk straight across and follow the path back into the woods. Do not leave the woods at the Merryland Close exit but continue just past this to the right, where you will find a gate through to Preston Fields.

Leave the park via Lower Penns Road, cross Torbay Road into Hilton Road and then take the third left into Cockington Lane, which becomes Old Paignton Road.

At the bottom of the dip in Old Paignton Road turn left into Scadson Woods. Stay on the path following the stream until you reach a clearly banked-up and culverted crossing point on your left. Cross over and at the top of a few steps take the right-hand path. Do not cross the next small wooden bridge, but carry straight on up through fields back to Occombe Farm.

WALK 10

Cockington Court.

With Saxon origins, Cockington, situated in a hidden valley and surrounded by rolling farmland and orchards, retains its rural identity. Within the centre of the village you can still see the smithy, mill, granary and weaver's cottage. Cockington Court sits a little way back from the village within a beautiful arboretum with a traditional cricket lawn in front of the house. Over the last thousand years three major families have controlled the court and estate. From 1130 to 1350 the land was owned by the Fitzmartin family, who took the surname De Cockington. It was

Old postcard of Cockington village.

the De Cockingtons who, in 1196, allowed stone to be quarried from Corbyn Head to build Torre Abbey. In 1375 the property was sold to the Cary family, who remained there until 1654. In 1521 William Cary, of the Cockington Carys, married Mary Boleyn, the sister of Henry VIII's second wife, Anne Boleyn, and thus became the uncle of the future Queen Elizabeth I when Anne gave birth in 1533. The last family who lived here, from just after the Civil War until the 1930s, was the Mallocks.

The Gamekeeper's Cottage is situated at the edge of Manscombe Woods. The building was first mentioned in 1517, when it was used by the warrener, who tended a colony of rabbits. Remains of a 2-mile wall built to surround the warren in 1659 can still be seen today. By Victorian times rabbits were no longer considered a luxury. The Cockington Estate employed a gamekeeper and woodland was planted to provide cover for pheasants.

Footpaths link the Cockington Estate to Scadson Woods. This area was open fields and orchards until approximately 1800, when two areas of woodland were planted. Old field boundaries and banks are still visible, including the ancient double bank that marked the Torquay/Paignton boundary. In 1878 Richard Mallock installed a system of leats and a reservoir to supply water to Cockington Valley. A hydram pump was used to get the water up over the hill and its remains can still be seen today. It is said that the Mallock family would wander down through the woods to their private beach at Hollicombe.

The second area of woodland to survive development due to its steep aspect is Occombe, meaning 'valley of the woods'. These woodlands boast ancient plant species, some wonderful old trees and an unusual claim to fame in that parts of the 1975 film *Monty Python and the Holy Grail* were filmed here!

Bluebells in Scadson Woods.

Occombe Farm

Both Occombe Valley and Scadson woods border the beautiful farmland of Occombe (right). This 150-acre organic farm is a mixture of pasture, wet meadows and woodland with a Site of Scientific Interest at its heart, containing important habitats and species that need to be protected. The farm includes a farm shop and café and is a good base for exploring the local area (visit www.occombe.org.uk).

Situated on Devon's rich and instantly recognisable red soils, the farm has remained unchanged, without being drained or subjected to extensive use of fertilisers, since the Second World War. As such, it represents an unusual snapshot of our country's farming past.

River
Dart

Galmpton Creek

Galmpton

GALMPTON CREEK

Churston Ferres

Start/Finish

WALK 11 – Galmpton Creek

Distance	7.6 miles (12.3km)
Estimated time	3½ hours
Difficulty	●●●○○
Ascent	874ft (266m)
Map	OS Explorer Map 110
Starting point	SX 896572

Notes: Although the route goes along streets and quiet roads in places, the footpaths away from the beaten track have some breathtaking views over Galmpton Creek in the middle and out across Tor Bay at the end. And who can resist Agatha Christie's house at Greenway, the River Dart from high above at Maypool, or Isambard Kingdom Brunel's railway viaduct? The walk crosses the beach very briefly at Galmpton Creek, so check the tide tables before you leave.

Starting from Broadsands car park, follow the footpath around the woodland to the south, to Broadsands Road. Stay with the road, beneath the railway line, until you come to the footpath on the left, leading to Bascombe Road. Reaching the road, walk a few yards to your right and then turn left onto the path, to the A3022. Turn left here, then right, onto Slade Lane, and stay with it to the end, turning onto Stoke Gabriel Road. Fork left onto Kiln Road and walk down to Dartside Quay.

Take the lane to the left, around the quay and past the boatyard, to travel uphill. Ignoring the turning to the left, take the footpath down to the creek, following it over the beach to the lime kiln, where it turns inland and travels up through two fields, passing between the farm buildings and onto the lane beyond. Note the chimney from the farm's one-time steam machinery. Crossing the lane, pick up the footpath on the other side, forking right

Galmpton Creek.

in the woods, towards Greenway. Follow the signs down to Greenway and to the ferry; or, if you are looping around back to Broadsands, turn left at the fingerpost at the end of the woods which points to Maypool/Kingswear/Brixham. (Retrace your steps to here if you are visiting Greenway first and turn right towards Maypool to rejoin the route.)

Follow the path around the fields and along the ancient green track, onto the road beyond. Turn right shortly after the youth hostel and take the footpath left a little further on. From here, take the next permissive path to the right, towards Kingswear, turning left almost immediately to walk to the A379. Cross the road and pick up the path opposite, bearing left to follow the path to Alston Lane and thence to the A3022. Cross this road onto Churston Road opposite, then take Church Lane, on the left a little way beyond. At the end of this lane, a footpath leads past the golf course and onto Churston Point. Turn left around the point and walk along the promenade at the end to return to the car park.

Galmpton Creek has been a boatbuilding centre for centuries and in its heyday over 300 sailing trawlers were built here, as well as wooden motor torpedo boats during the Second World War. It is still a bustling marine repair centre, but it is used nowadays mostly by pleasure craft.

The lime kiln on the beach is one of several scattered along the estuary foreshore and limestone from the quarry across the creek was burned here to produce a soil fertiliser.

Lime kiln at Galmpton Creek.

The area from Berry Head sits on a thick bed of Devonian limestone, once marine reefs, and Galmpton was an important centre for quarrying the stone on the River Dart. It was also used as ballast in the early ships sailing from here to Newfoundland, and Galmpton Creek limestone has been found in some of the earliest buildings in North America. It also appears in French and Spanish harbours for the same reason.

Greenway has a rich history with many seafaring connections, as you might expect from its waterside location. At the time of its first mention, in 1493, 'Greynway' was an important crossing point of the Dart, as it still is today. The first Greenway house was a Tudor mansion, built here in the late sixteenth century for Otho and Katherine Gilbert. Their son, Sir Humphrey, was a favourite with Elizabeth I, as was his stepbrother Sir Walter Raleigh. In searching for the North-West Passage, Gilbert stumbled across Newfoundland and took it for the Queen. In the eighteenth century another house was built at Greenway (the central block of the current building), and its owner, Roope Harris Roope, was a noted seafarer who developed trading links with the New World. It was he who imported plants such as camellias and seeds, laying the foundations for the landscape gardening which later made Greenway famous.

Subsequent owners of the house devoted much time and money to the gardens, creating, by the middle of the nineteenth century, 'a park of much natural beauty' giving 'the appearance of enchantment rather than reality'. It is hardly surprising, then, that when the railway arrived the incumbent of the time – a Cornish copper magnate – fiercely resisted the proposal to run the line over Greenway to carry passengers to the Dart. A compromise was reached, and the Paignton–Dartmouth Steam Railway still runs through the tunnel that was constructed beneath Greenway. In 1938 a certain Mr and Mrs Mallowan bought the house as a holiday home. Both were keen gardeners and passionate about Greenway's horticultural abundance. Mr Mallowan was a noteworthy archaeologist and his wife was none other than crime writer Agatha Christie. Greenway was the setting for her book *Dead Man's Folly*, even down to the boathouse where Marlene Tucker's body was found.

WALK 11

Steam railway crossing Brunel's viaduct.

Brixham

The
Grove

Marriage Woods

Elberr
Cove

Churston
Point

Start/Finish

P

Walk 12 – Broadsands to Churston Cove

Distance	3.6miles (5.8km)
Estimated time	1½ hours
Difficulty	••• ••
Ascent	276ft (84m)
Map	OS Explorer Map 110
Starting point	SX 895574

Notes: This walk is a beautiful mix of woodland and sheltered coves. In particular Elberry Cove, where Lord Churston created a nineteenth-century sea-water bathing house, today a rather romantic ruin.

From Broadsands car park head out towards the beach and follow the promenade around and up onto Churston Point. Follow the coastline and then through the gate towards Elberry Cove. Take the left-hand path down some steps to cross the beach.

At the southern end of the beach follow the South West Coast Path as it rises steeply into Marriage Woods and onwards to Fishcombe Point, where steps descend to the picturesque Churston Cove. From here cross the beach to where another set of steps rise into The Grove woodland. Continue on the path up through the woods, at the end of which you will pass through stone gateposts and along a stone wall. This very ancient trackway, possibly 3,000 to 4,000 years old, links the coast to the South Hams inland. At the end of the lane turn right and then right again into Church Lane. At the end of this lane, a footpath leads across the golf course and runs adjacent to fields at the back of Elberry Cove. Where the path splits either walk back around the headland of Churston Point or follow Elberry Lane past Elberry Farm, which was built in Victorian times, to Broadsands.

WALK 12

The Grove

Fishcombe Point

BRIXHAM HARBOUR

P Start/Finish

Breakwater
Beach

Shoalstone
Pool

Walk 13 – Brixham Harbour

Distance	3.5 miles (5.6km)
Estimated time	1 ½ hours
Difficulty	● · · · ·
Ascent	36ft (12m)
Map	OS Explorer Map 110
Starting point	SX 924568

Notes: This walk along Brixham's harbour waterfront takes in all the sights, sounds and heritage that make up the life of this famous fishing port. Aside from the extension beyond the breakwater towards Shoalstone, the walk is level and paved throughout, thus being suitable for wheelchairs.

Starting at Freshwater Quarry car park, with the sea on your left walk along the edge of the outer harbour, a mix of pavement and boardwalk, towards the busy inner harbour area, passing under the Brixham Yacht Club and towards the newly regenerated Fish Quay. A stroll out along New Quay provides a fascinating short detour with a chance to view some of the modern trawlers and the fishermen at work. Continue around the inner harbour, under the old fish market and past the statue of William of Orange towards Brixham Marina, from where it is possible to stroll the full length of the breakwater, which provides great views looking back towards Brixham and of course out across the bay. Follow the same route back to the car park.

If you wish to extend the walk, turn left at the inner end of the breakwater onto Breakwater Beach, where steps lead up to Berry Head Road. Turn left and follow the road along to the junction with the footpath to Shoalstone. The shoreline just past Shoalstone Pool is geologically very interesting

WALK 13

Brixham breakwater.

and you can download a guided walk for this area from www.englishrivierageopark.org.uk. Retrace your steps to return to the start. Or, if you are still feeling energetic, it is only a short walk along the Coast Path to Berry Head.

The history of Brixham goes back over 1,000 years and its role as a fishing port is mentioned in the Domesday Book. The name evolved from the Saxon 'Brioc's Ham' (*ham* meaning village, estate or home, preceded by the name of the person who founded the settlement or an important person who lived there), to Briseham in 1086 and Brikkesham by 1285. In medieval times the port had a strong trade in drying fish and curing pilchards, recorded as taking place in 1500. Brixham was by this time a town of two communities: 'Fish Town', clustered around the harbour, and 'Cow Town', the area of higher Brixham largely associated with farming.

The port became renowned as a safe anchorage, nestling under the protective

Brixham quay.

limestone arm of Berry Head. It was here that William of Orange landed in 1688 before advancing on London to claim the British throne. Later, during the Napoleonic Wars, the Channel Fleet would replenish its supplies under the protection of the guns of Berry Head's fortifications.

The last major extension to enclose the harbour and provide improved shelter was the outer breakwater, completed in 1916. Over half a mile (one kilometre) in length, it required a considerable amount of stone, which was provided by the nearby Freshwater Quarry, on the opposite side of the outer harbour.

The Reverend Henry Lyte creates a link between all aspects of Brixham. Reverend Lyte settled in the parish of Lower Brixham in 1823, taking residence in what is now the Berry Head Hotel. He would preach to the fisherman before they set sail and would support the community while the men were at sea. In his spare time his love of geology led him to explore the caves of Brixham from about 1840. Brixham Cavern in particular, discovered in 1858, was to play an important role alongside Kents Cavern in Torquay when excavations carried out by William Pengelly revealed important vertebrate remains such as mammoth, woolly rhinoceros and cave lion, finally convincing geologists of the antiquity of man and his coexistence with extinct animals.

Brixham Sails

Considerable amounts of iron ore and associated mineral iron ochre were discovered in the limestone around Brixham. In Victorian times a local businessman used the ochre to develop the first rust-resistant paint. By the time the paintworks took the name of the Tor Bay Paint Co. in 1895, it was exporting all over the world. Among the contracts held by the company, the paint was used in the maintenance of the Victoria Falls Bridge on the Zambezi River.

The same red-coloured ochre was used in a process to help preserve the sails of the Brixham trawlers (above), making them more water-resistant and giving them their recognisable red colour.

St Mary's Bay

Durl Head

Mew Stone

BERRY HEAD

P Start/Finish

Berry Head

Walk 14 – Berry Head

Distance	3.5 miles (5.6km)
Estimated time	1½ hours
Difficulty	● ● ● ● ●
Ascent	151ft (46m)
Map	OS Explorer Map 110
Starting point	SX 941562

Notes: Berry Head is a National Nature Reserve and one of the major gateway sites for the English Riviera Global Geopark. The headland and the surrounding fields are grazed by livestock, so please keep dogs under control and be prepared for some stiles to climb over, gates to close and cattle grids. The path goes near to the cliff edge at times and there are drops from the fort walls, so take great care. Allow more time if you intend to stop for refreshments at the café. Berry Head is one of the many countryside sites in the South-West where you can hire a mobility scooter to explore. See www.countrysidemobility.org for details.

From the far end of the Berry Head car park follow the tarmac road up onto the headland and bear right into the North Fort. Once through the formidable fort entrance, head to the right to enjoy the new interpretation centre and café. Opposite the centre, a look over the fort walls provides a great view into the massive quarry below and out across Tor Bay. It is possible to reach the end of the headland by walking along the central road past the Cold War bunker on the right and then the Artillery Store and lighthouse on the left, but be warned, the end of the headland is not fenced and it is a 60-metre (200-foot) drop down to the sea. From the lighthouse follow the path along the southern edge of the headland for inspiring views towards the Mew Stone and Cod Rock. The path leads towards the back of the interpretation centre, where a bird hide nestles against the edge of the cliff, a protected spot from where the seabirds and guillemot colony can be viewed.

Once back through the north fort entrance, veer left away from the tarmac road to pick up a path through scrub towards the South Fort. A quick detour up into the fort over the recently restored bridge provides spectacular views. From here the Coast Path hugs the landward side of the southern fort and then continues along the cliff top past Durl Head, with views of Sharkham Point. As you reach the housing leave the Coast Path and turn right, following the footpath along the edge of the housing to Gillard Road. Turn right again along the road to return to the car park.

The impressive promontory of Berry Head, towering above the English Channel, has long protected our nation, particularly in times of war. Yet, long before the construction of the Second World War and Cold War observation posts and anti-aircraft guns, eighteenth and nineteenth century signalling stations or the Napoleonic forts, our earliest ancestors found protection from wild animals and weather in a network of caves beneath the limestone headland.

The quarry on the northern flank is the culmination of over 300 years of quarrying.

Seal with a mackerel dinner.

It was in use during Napoleonic times the most obvious products being visible in the ramparts of the two Napoleonic forts, for which the headland is designated a scheduled ancient monument. Ironically more than half of the original fort was lost to later phases of workings. The quarry was in its heyday during the 1930s, 40s and 50s, with production in some years approaching 200,000 tons. The great purity of the limestone (nearly 99 per cent calcium carbonate) has long made Berry Head important to agriculture, industry and construction. So extensive are the quarry workings that in places the floor of the quarry is actually below sea level. Quarry workers uncovered a network of caves and passages that wind their way into the heart of the headland. Today the quiet seclusion of the quarry makes it ideal for nesting seabirds and hunting peregrine falcons, while the caves are home to a colony of the rare greater horseshoe bats.

Berry Head ranger monitoring the guillemot colony.

Berry Head Nature Reserve

With a variety of habitats the grasslands, woodlands and cliffs are home or a stop-off point for about 200 species of birds. These include the guillemot, which chooses to lay its single egg on exposed rocky ledges rather than build a nest. The cliffs are host to the largest colony of guillemots on the south coast.

A popular spot for seals, the sea caves, rocky inlets and waters around the headland teem with colourful marine creatures such as sea anemones, urchins, brittle star and rare corals. The height of the headland provides a great vantage point from which to watch for bottlenose dolphins, harbour porpoises and basking sharks. Yet the tiny plants beneath your feet are probably the most precious such as the Bee orchid (right). The flower-rich limestone grassland found here is a real rarity, with a community of plants found nowhere else in Britain. Clinging to the thin limestone soils are around 500 plant species, a good number of them unique.

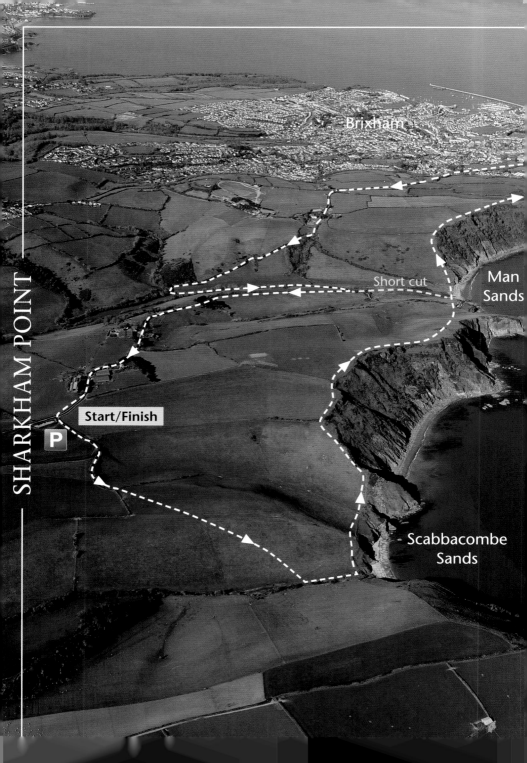

SHARKHAM POINT

Brixham

Man
Sands

Short cut

Start/Finish

P

Scabbacombe
Sands

Berry Head

Sharkham Point

WALK 15 – Sharkham Point

Distance	5.9 miles (9.5km)
Estimated time	3½ hours
Difficulty	● ● ● ● ○
Ascent	1,332ft (406m)
Map	OS Explorer Map OL20
Starting point	SX 911522

Notes: A strenuous walk with some steep ascents and descents, nonetheless this is not to be missed, with a wealth of wild flowers, a tiny and remote sandy cove, and a wetland nature reserve. Take advantage of the spectacular views along the coast in both directions to catch your breath, and if you want a shortened version, use Woodhuish Lane or Mansands Lane beyond it to return to the car park from Man Sands.

From the Scabbacombe Lane car park, take the track heading south-east around two fields and then forking right to drop diagonally down towards Scabbacombe Sands. Turn left onto the South West Coast Path and follow it as it rollercoasters to the tiny cove at Man Sands, one of the country's fastest-changing habitats.

Stay with the Coast Path as it climbs steeply up to Southdown Cliff and onto the headland at Sharkham Point. Around the point, turn left onto St Mary's Road. Walk past the campsite, picking up Yards Lane just beyond the second campsite road. Bear right, then left at Chiseldon Hill, to Southdown Cross. Turn left onto Southdown Road and bear left at the farm, then after 200 yards turn right onto Mill Lane. Continue for about three quarters of a mile, ignoring the footpath on the left, until it ends at a T-junction. Turn left and go past the car park to Woodhuish Lane. Turn right onto the road and follow it past Woodhuish Farm and back to Scabbcombe Lane car park.

WALK 15

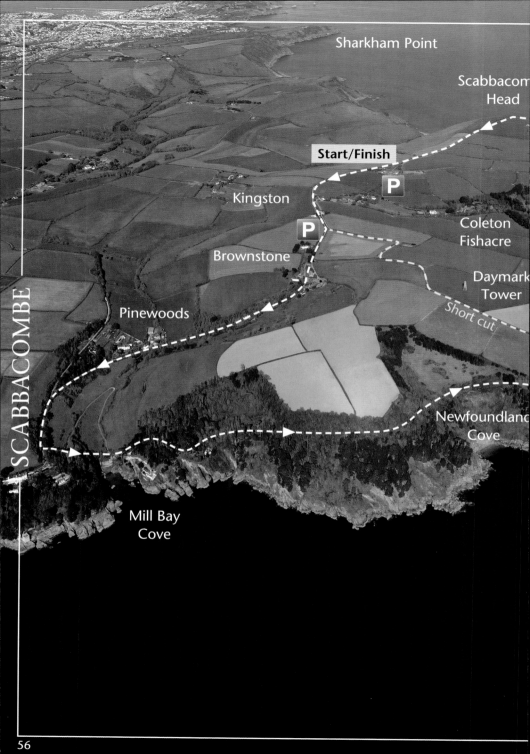

Sharkham Point

Scabbacom
Head

Start/Finish

Kingston

Coleton
Fishacre

Daymark
Tower

Short cut

Brownstone

Pinewoods

SCABBACOMBE

Newfoundland
Cove

Mill Bay
Cove

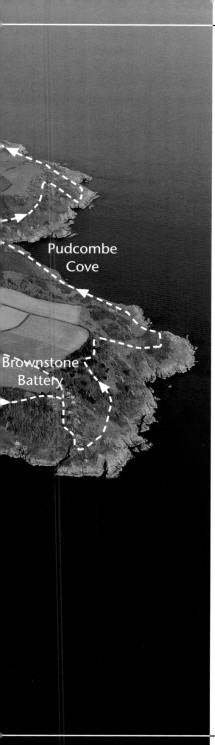

Pudcombe
Cove

Brownstone
Battery

WALK 16 – Scabbacombe

Distance	5.75 miles (9.3km)
Estimated time	3 hours
Difficulty	● ● ● ● ○
Ascent	1,352ft (412m)
Map	OS Explorer Map OL20
Starting point	SX 910513

Notes: This is a fairly strenuous walk, with a lot of ascents and descents, and in places the path is narrow and steep. There are stunning views along the coast in both directions, a fascinating journey through the remnants of a Second World War battery and a nature reserve passing the National Trust property at Coleton Fishacre.

Turn left after Kingston to get to the car park. Take the lane westwards to the road beyond. Continuing in the same direction, go left on the lane and then the path, ignoring the paths to the left, and stay with it past Brownstone and Pinewoods. Turn left onto the steps at the top of Warren Wood, then take the South West Coast Path into the valley and around Mill Bay Cove.

The path climbs more steps to the woodland at the top (a nature reserve), before continuing to the Brownstone Battery. Take the steps leading downhill from the lookout and follow the path around the coast as it zigzags back up, then turn right at the top to go eastwards to Pudcombe Cove. Here a path leads inland through Coleton Fishacre, but carry on along the Coast Path as it climbs the far side of the cove and continues around the coast for about a mile and a half. Ignoring the path inland on the way, turn left onto the path leading inland as Scabbacombe Sands come into view below and follow it back up to the start of the walk.

WALK 16

Coleton Fishacre was built in the 1920s by the D'Oyly Carte family (of opera fame) as a holiday home. The design of the house was influenced by the Art Deco style of the Jazz Age and visitors to the National Trust property are played excerpts from Gilbert and Sullivan to celebrate the family's connections with the operatic duo. The 30-acre garden lies in a moist and sheltered valley and is planted with many exotic species from the Mediterranean, South Africa and New Zealand, which thrive here.

The entrance to the estate is to the north of the property, near the start of the walk, and access to the gardens from the Coast Path is not normally permitted except to members of the Trust.

Brownstone Battery was built in 1940 as a Close Defence Site, designed to stop enemy forces landing on nearby beaches at Slapton Sands or Blackpool Sands and to destroy any beachhead the Germans might try and establish there. It was known that Hitler was planning to invade Britain, and Brownstone Battery was an integral part of the defence against this land invasion. Dartmouth was seen as being particularly vulnerable to attack. As well as being an important port in its own right, it was frequently used by the navy and had a motor torpedo boat installation. It also had anti-submarine nets at the mouth of the estuary and a military boat-repairing facility at Philips Shipyard at nearby Noss Creek.

Coleton Camp, at the car park to the north of Coleton Fishacre, was also an important part of this defence strategy. It was operated by the Royal Air Force as part of its RDF (or radar) chain, and was also built in 1940 to provide cover for Lyme Bay and Start Bay and for the Channel as a whole. Its exposed hilltop position gave it excellent 360-degree visibility.

Towards Scabbacombe
Head from Sharkham Point.

Brownstone Battery gun position.

Man Sands.

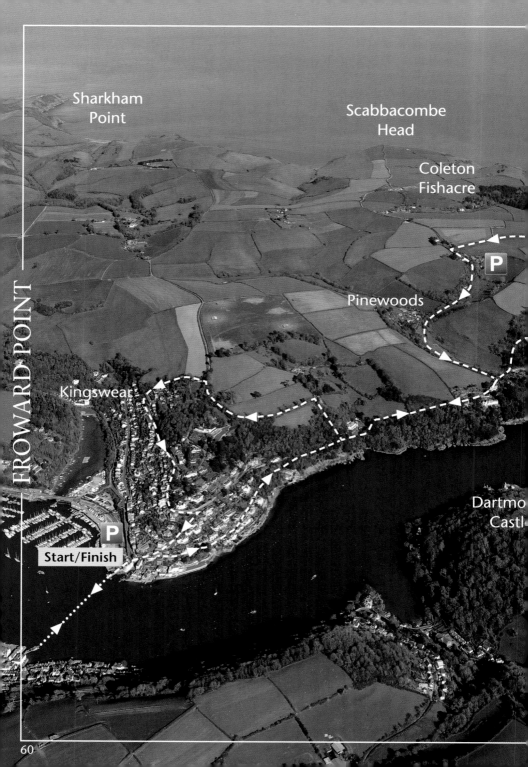

Sharkham Point

Scabbacombe Head

Coleton Fishacre

Pinewoods

P

Kingswear

FROWARD POINT

Dartmo Castl

P

Start/Finish

Daymark Tower

Froward Point

Bay
ove

WALK 17 – Froward Point

Distance	5 miles (8km)
Estimated time	2½ hours
Difficulty	● ● ● ● ○
Ascent	1,071ft (326m)
Map	OS Explorer Map OL20
Starting point	SX 881510

Notes: The walk starts and ends at Kingswear. Give yourself time to take the ferry across to Dartmouth afterwards and wander around the historic seventeenth-century Butterwalk, the fifteenth-century castle and the famous Bayard's Cove, from where two crusades and the Pilgrim Fathers' Mayflower *set sail. Or take a ride up the valley on the steam railway for stunning views of the Dart Valley.*

From the ferry, take the road uphill and follow the South West Coast Path through the archway on the right a little further on, carrying on up Alma Steps. At the top turn right onto Beacon Road and follow it around above the river as it narrows to a small lane and then descends to Inverdart. After about half a mile the lane turns inland. Keep to the Coast Path and after a short while take the timber steps steeply down into Warren Wood and follow the path to Mill Bay. Another set of steep steps ascending here leads you into a nature reserve, where you follow the path for about a mile and a half through pinewoods. As the path levels out there are views out over Start Bay, before it curves around the back of Newfoundland Cove and ascends to a clearing surrounded by the remnants of the Second World War Brownstone Battery (see Walk 16).

From the clearing pick up the military road

WALK 17

A view of the rugged coastline at Froward.

leading due north, uphill, past the daymark tower and on to the T-junction above Brownstone (ignore the turning to the right towards the top). Turn left at the top and follow the path as it climbs up to Pinewoods past Higher Brownstone and then curves around to pass the top of the steps to Mill Bay. Retrace your steps north-westwards, towards Kingswear, then take the footpath leading off to the right about three-quarters of a mile later, following it sharply left and then right and left again before it meets Mount Ridley Road. Here turn right and take the footpath left after a short distance. Turn left on the road beyond and follow it downhill and back to the start of the walk in Kingswear.

Dartmouth Castle was built in 1388 by John Hawley, who was the Mayor of Dartmouth and the inspiration for Chaucer's 'Shipman' in *The Canterbury Tales*. A few years earlier, Edward IV had offered 30 pounds a year for ever if the town were to build a 'tower with a chain sufficient in length and strength to stretch across the mouth of the haven'. A century or so later, the 'gun tower' was added, thought to be the first fortification in England to be built to accommodate heavy 'ship-sinking' cannon. Henry VIII added open-air gun platforms, and it was added to yet again in the seventeenth century as military technology advanced.

It was besieged for a month during the English Civil War before it was taken by the Royalists, who built an earthwork fort at Gallant's Bower, above, and by this means were able to protect it for three years, before the Roundheads took it. It continued as a working fort through the nineteenth century and the Gun Battery from that time remained in use throughout the First and Second World Wars.

Dartmouth Castle.

Daymark Tower

Buoys are often used as navigational marks, but in some places the tides can be so fierce and the weather so severe that the buoys are easily swept away and an alternative has to be found. Sometimes this is small and easily improvised, like a withy or a perch planted in the water in a small river or creek. Clearly a major waterway like the Dart Estuary needed something a little more prominent and permanent and in 1864 the Dartmouth Harbour Commissioners built the daymark to guide mariners to the harbour entrance. The hollow stone tower is 80 feet tall (25 metres) and is visible from a long way out to sea. It is a Grade 2 listed building.

Kingswear Castle, this side of the river, was built shortly after Dartmouth Castle to support the defence of the river and was completed in 1502. Within fifty years, however, Kingswear Castle was redundant and it fell into disrepair, until Charles Seale Hayne, businessman and Liberal MP for Ashburton, bought it in 1855 and refurbished it as a summer residence. Seal Hayne was the first chairman of the Dartmouth and Torbay Railway.

When approaching from the sea, the mouth of the Dart Estuary is not obvious until you are very close to it. The Mew Stone Rock, lying off Froward Point, can be seen easily when approaching from the west, but not from the south.

For dates and times for the Steam Railway (which usually operates April–October), contact 01803 555872 or visit www.dartmouthrailriver.co.uk.

Daymark tower above Froward Point.

Collecting Code

The geology of the English Riviera is special and vulnerable. Please follow our Collecting Code (www.englishrivierageopark.org.uk) and in particular:

- Please do not hammer or dig at any site without permission
- Please do not remove any fossils, rocks or minerals which are still embedded

Safety Messages

People following the trails and walks do so at their own risk, so when out and about enjoying the walks always remember to stay safe:

- Learn to read a map to be able to accurately report your position in the event of an emergency – visit www.ordnancesurvey.co.uk
- Plan a walk that suits your fitness level
- Always tell someone where you are going and how long you expect to be gone
- If intending to explore the shoreline always check the tide timetables before you go out
- Take the relevant OS map with you on your walk

- Wear sensible shoes and be prepared for any weather
- Be aware that the surface of the Coast Path varies and will generally be more natural and more uneven away from car parks, towns and villages
- If you leave the coast path to explore the beaches and coves keep an eye on the incoming tide as it is easy to get trapped, especially around the headlands
- Beware of large waves in rough weather
- Stay away from the base of cliffs – rockfalls can happen at any time
- While walking the coast path keep away from cliff edges
- For their safety, ensure your children and dogs are under control
- Be considerate and follow the Countryside Code
- If visiting by boat or taking to the water, the English Riviera Harbour Guide will provide you with relevant information and safety advice (www.tor-bay-harbour.co.uk)

If you have enjoyed these walks and would like to find out more about the rest of the 630 miles of the South West Coast Path National Trail visit www.southwestcoastpath.com.

To find out more about the English Riviera Global Geopark visit www.englishrivierageopark.org.uk.

To discover more about other Global Geoparks visit www.europeangeoparks.org or www.globalgeopark.org.

In an emergency dial 999 or 112 and ask for the coastguard.